All thanks be to my Lord and Saviour Jesus Christ,
For all His love, grace, guidance and provision.

And to my beautiful and loving wife, Doreen,
For all her love, support and belief in me.

ISBN 978-981-09-2420-1

"Teach a man to fish and you feed him for a lifetime; Give a student the reason to learn and he will never forget what you taught him."

Contents

The Philosophy

"Begin with the end in mind."

Why did you pick up this book? What are you hoping to get out of it? What happens if you don't get what you expect?

In as much as you would feel cheated if your expectations were not met, children face the same issue. They are put into classes not of their choosing, engaged in activities not of their liking, studying subjects not of their interest. So it is little wonder then why some children would rather spend time in the arcades.

Would you, spend 8 hours a day, 5 days a week, 40 weeks a year, doing something you don't like, around people who criticise you? Some of us do; our jobs. But why should children put themselves through this? What can we do to make learning more meaningful and therefore more effective for them?

In the course of this book, I hope to take us on a journey through the common learning experience and provide suggestions on how we can ease the points of tension between the educator and child, in the hope that we can better understand what children go through and help them make meaning of their learning.

How we learn

There is much literature to suggest that learning occurs on the 40:40:40 rule. This rule posits the view that there are some things we commit to short term memory and others to long term memory. Let me illustrate.

Think back to a significant incident in your childhood.

Here are some questions to consider;
What do you remember?
Why do you remember it?
What did that incident mean to you?
Has it shaped the way you do things today?
Has it shaped the way you relate to other people?
What did the experience teach you about yourself?

The experience probably did not happen in a classroom. If it did, it probably was not a deliberate part of a teacher's lesson plan. But the experience stuck, the learning was committed to the long term memory. That is the important thing.

If we can distil the essence of that experience and translate it into meaningful learning experiences for our children, we would have a good chance of constructing learning experiences that will be committed to the child's long term memory. So let's see why the experience stuck.

Why the experience stuck

The experience, and all the consequent learning, stuck because the event was meaningful to us. It could have been a first experience, it could have involved people close to us or it could have resulted in a life choice that we are living with even till today. Regardless, that experience, for one reason or another, became meaningful to us and that made us commit it to our long term memory.

In the same way, we as educators; teachers and parents alike; hold sway over those very same facets of our children's lives and therefore are able to greatly influence what they commit to their long and short term memories. Here's why.

First experiences are important

Teens are often said to have emotional baggage, and rightly so. In their 13 to 19 years, the people they have come into contact with have given them many first experiences which have shaped their lives, much like what that experience did for you.

Think back; were the actors in your recount deliberate in creating that experience for you? Did they realise the impact they were leaving on you? This is the importance that learning experiences have, what more first experiences.

Teachers often overlook introductions and pass them off as lead-ins. This cannot be further from the truth. If their first experience of a subject disinterests the children, they would have little impetus to commit their time and energies to giving you a second chance. So how great your influence if you are introducing something to a child for the first time.

What we do and say influence their learning

What we do and say, or even don't do or don't say, guide our children down life's road by either opening or closing doors of opportunity for them.

Go back again to that experience. How much of what was said to you was deliberately and purposefully trying to send the message that it did? Did the actors even mean what they said? Regardless, did it change the way you viewed yourself? Did it change the way you viewed and related to others?

If we have a close relationship with our children, our influence in their lives is great. How we position education, learning, subjects, topics, is therefore all the more vital in either imbuing or killing the interest in our children.

Don't we find that our children, when they were young, take best to things that we ourselves are interested in? As teachers, don't we often find that our closest students pick up our lingo, emulate our demeanours? Even those we are unconscious of ourselves? So if we position a subject to our children as merely something they need to know to get by and pass their exams, we will be conditioning them to park all the information into the first 40; the 40 days or weeks; the short term memory.

Give them a reason to learn
The intrinsic must come from the extrinsic. For many of us, the reason for learning first came from the extrinsic value of either, getting rewarded in kind for our grades; or the promise of a scholarship; or in my case, avoiding my mother's cane.

So children must be given a good reason to learn; hopefully, a reason more meaningful and with greater consequences than the latest game console. This will help them develop their own intrinsic values to learning; values spawned from their developed love for the subject or skill.

We should also reward our students each and every time they step into our classrooms because they chose to give us their time; a scarce and non-renewable commodity, and for some, one with a very high opportunity cost. They do this because they believe that we can give them something meaningful in return. And the best reward would be a reason for learning that is relevant, something they can use immediately to enrich their daily lives.

This is even more imperative for involuntary learners. To win over 'wayward' children, we need to compete with their other pursuits, which give them greater satisfaction and hence greater meaning and motivation for engaging in them. So all the more we need to deliberately convey what we want them to know and crucially why it should matter to them.

Let me illustrate with this example.

Suppose you are a math teacher teaching algebra. We begin by asking ourselves why students should spend time mucking about with letters that are supposed to represent numbers. Why not give them the numbers and be done with it? What is the true purpose of algebra in their lives?

Any mathematician will tell you that algebra is needed to solve for unknowns. So instead of telling them the answer to $\cos30°=x$, why not pose them a problem like this;
'Suppose your neighbourhood suffered a sea level rise of 1m. Would your home still be around?'

With the question, we get the students interested in where they live, what is around them, how far away they are from the sea. After figuring that out, we then get them to work out the angle of elevation from the sea to their homes. Take the cosine value of the angle of elevation, and imputing the 1m sea level rise, they will then be able to work out just how much land will be lost by sea level rise and therefore, whether their homes will still be around when Jonny Polar Bear loses his last bastion.

Some call this authentic learning. I call this rewarding the children with something meaningful. Letting them walk out of time spent with you, with something from their prescribed learning which they can use to enrich their lives.

Translating it into a plan

In order to achieve all that has been discussed earlier, we must begin with the end in mind and distil the purpose of our teaching. Why should the children give us their time? What is so important about this topic that the students really need to know? How will it enrich their lives? The plan has to be conscious and deliberate in answering these questions, in order to ensure that the learning experience is meaningful and rewarding.

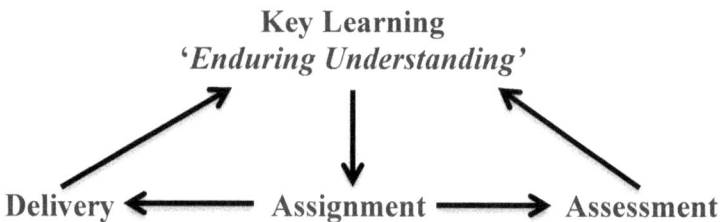

Key Learning
'Enduring Understanding'

Delivery ← Assignment → Assessment

To this end, the concept of Enduring Understandings from Wiggins and McTighe gives us a useful starting point.

The Key Learning, or Enduring Understanding, has to be knowledge that is relevant and will stay relevant to the children long after they have left the classroom. How the learning is delivered, reinforced and assessed, must deliberately, consciously and purposefully, bring the child to the intended Key Learning.

After establishing the Key Learning, we then select the assignment which best allows the children to practice the skills learnt or apply the knowledge taught. It could be work done away from or in the classroom. It could be collaborative or done alone. Regardless, it has to allow a measurable performance of the knowledge or skill.

At the same time, we need to know that learning has effectively taken place. To achieve this, we need to be very clear about what has been taught. If it is a skill, the assessment must provide a platform to perform that skill. If it is content, the assessment must provide a platform that showcases the knowledge acquired.

Once we know what assignment and assessment we want to use, we can then select the activity which best allows for these to take place. Note that this is done only AFTER deciding what to teach, how to reinforce and how to assess. The activity chosen can allow for knowledge to be discovered or teacher delivered. Regardless of the form, the learning goals should determine the learning activity; the activity should never dictate the learning.

Finally, we need to make sense of the information derived from the assessment to help inform on the learning that has taken place. How do we know if the children ended up with the desired Key Learning? What does a score of 50 in a 100 mark test mean? Only by making sense of the results can we be sure that the learning has been accomplished.

In the end, teaching cannot be incidental. Children need to learn in a deliberate manner, receiving explicitly the value of what they are learning, seeing that their learning is meaningful to them. Only by so doing can their learning experiences be effective.

So what have you learnt? Has this experience been meaningful?

Exercise

Raise a subject, topic, area or skill that concerns you.

Why does it concern you?

Is it because the students don't seem to want to pay attention?

Is it because the students seem to be able to learn the content in class but are not able to reproduce their learning when it comes time for the exam?

What do they really need to know in this subject, or skill?

What is really important that will help them later on in life?

Why is it so important?

Exercise - Analysis

Why does it concern you?
Is it because the students don't seem to want to pay attention?

This is probably the most difficult point of tension to resolve, motivation. Nonetheless, there are some things that we can do.

Mode of Transmission
One common cause of low intrinsic motivation is teaching in a manner that shows no relevance of the subject to their daily lives. Children exhibit a lack of interest due to the fact that they don't feel they've gained any knowledge that is **immediately useful** to them. Let me give you an illustration.

In teaching students the topic of adverbs, I could either deliver the knowledge myself, or let them discover what adverbs are.

In the former, I tell them what adverbs are; give them a list of adverbs to memorise; then have them fill out a worksheet which requires them to complete sentences using adverbs. Incidentally, this worksheet will essentially be a variation on the test which they will sit for 3 weeks later. Their test scores from 3 weeks later should then tell me how well they have learnt adverbs. Or will it?

If the test score says 100%, does it mean that the students have understood the application of adverbs; when and how to use them; or have I just checked their ability to memorise the placement of a set list of words in a given context?

Instead, if I employed the latter method and began by telling them the concept of adverbs; words that describe the manner of actions; gave them examples from books, and then got them to comment on their classmates actions in a role-play using adverbs, not only will that teach them the concept of adverbs but also give them a meaningful and immediate application of adverbs, one which can be useful to them right away.

The assignment now becomes the activity which requires them to use adverbs to describe their classmate. And if you are concerned with the child's ability to cope with exam-type questions, you could still have a timed test as the assessment of their learning. But this time, because the knowledge has become meaningful to them through immediate application, not only will they **know** what adverbs really are and **understand** how to use them, this **knowledge will reside in their long term memory**.

Make Learning Explicit
Students with lower academic ability often find it difficult to deal with knowledge. Their natural compunction when overwhelmed is to shut down, shut out and stop paying attention to the lesson. When this happens, what they are really saying is,
"Whoa there, I can't take it anymore, time-out."

Such students need to be explicitly told the Key Learning first thing in the lesson, so that even when they become overwhelmed, the Key Learning is not lost.

Going back to the adverb example, begin by telling them what adverbs are, what they do and how to use them. Do this in the first 5 minutes and then carry on with the activities planned for the day, safe in the knowledge that these children have already had their learning taken care of.

The solutions discussed above do presuppose that we have already derived the intended Key Learning for the lesson. How long the

Key Learning will be retained for, hinges on our reason for them to be acquiring the learning.

If we believe that there is a useful application to everything they learn, we should be helping our children see the relevance of their prescribed knowledge in their daily lives. The moment they realise that they are walking away with something which they could immediately use, it will improve their motivation and retention.

Is it because the students seem to be able to learn the content in class but are not able to reproduce their learning when it comes time for the exam?

Many teachers pay little attention to this aspect of learning. They assume that just because the child has been told something many times, the child is able to apply that truth to other circumstances. Here is an example.

Assume I tell you the following;
1 + 1 = 2
2 + 1 = 3

And then I ask you for the answer to 3 + 1.

If you had no knowledge of the concept that is numeracy, you too wouldn't have the faintest idea what the answer would be.

When trying to understand a child's lack of ability in cross situational application of knowledge and skills, we first need to check what we have delivered, and then make sure that the different situations in the assessment or assignment checks for that very same thing. In this respect, the onus is very much on us the educator, not the child.

What do they really need to know in this subject, or skill?
What is really important that will help them later on in life?
Why is it so important?

Wiggins and McTighe call them Enduring Understandings. I call them, the purpose for learning. Regardless, these are truths which should matter to the students long after they have stepped out of school. Just what they are, will be dealt with in the next chapter.

But suffice to say that we need to think about what they are learning and just why that is important to them. If we ourselves can't answer that question, then how can we expect children, who know no better, to commit their time and energies to learning it?

Also, the more things we can put in this category of Key Learning, the easier it will be for students to learn and retain the information in the realm of the last 40 in the 40:40:40 rule, 40 years, the long term memory. And this is really what we want to aim for when we educate our children.

What do they really need to know?

"Think for the child by thinking from the child."

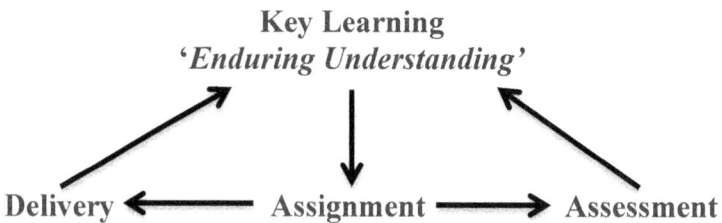

Key Learning
'Enduring Understanding'

Delivery ← — **Assignment** → **Assessment**

We begin building the learning experience by looking at the first aspect, the Key Learning.

As mentioned in the previous chapter, the main condition for an effective learning experience is that every aspect of that experience must bring the children to the intended Key Learning. How the lesson is delivered, how the learning is reinforced, even how the learning is assessed, must all; deliberately, consciously and purposefully; point the children to the truth to be acquired.

But before we craft the Key Learning, we must first understand the context in which the learning is going to take place. This can be uncovered by examining **Subject, Level and Duration**.

Subject, Level, Duration
These are often glossed over by educators. But if insufficient care is put into these components, we will never be able to promote long term retention of learning. Let me explain.

Subject
This item is often copied out from a textbook or a scheme of work as being the next item in line to go into the teaching framework. But if we do not purposefully distil the important and meaningful knowledge from the subject that we want to convey, it will get lost in transmission. Let me give you an illustration.

Subject: Plate Tectonics (Volcanoes)

Geographers will no doubt be aware that the subject of Plate Tectonics is vast, covering plate movement, to crustal composition, to earthquakes. Merely narrowing it down to 'volcanoes' still does not bring to the fore the important knowledge which we feel the students must acquire. What about volcanoes do we think is so vitally important that the students must know; their process of formation, their impact on humans?

Subject: Plate Tectonics (Impact of volcanoes on man)

In this second example, we are not looking to limit the coverage of the lesson. Instead, we are selecting the truly important knowledge from the subject for the students, so that we will be able to distil the relevant and meaningful Key Learning later on.

Subject: Plate Tectonics (Volcanoes: Why they happen, how they happen & what they mean to us)

This third example shows us that the scope of knowledge to be covered can be widened without compromising the clarity. This is especially important if we are trying to plan learning experiences that cover a wider area of knowledge.

So from here we see that it is of utmost importance to clearly define the intended subject area. This is the first step to crafting meaningful and relevant Key Learning for our children.

Level

Being conscious of the level that our children are in not only helps us determine the appropriacy of the language, the depth of content, possible schema that may already exist, but more importantly, the things that the child finds meaningful and relevant.

Extend this one step further to include the geographical location and socio-economic background of the child, and now you have an excellent picture of who you are trying to enthuse and more importantly, educate. Let me give you an illustration.

15 year old children, with lower socio-economic status, living in urban centres far away from tectonic plate boundaries, won't give two hoots about earthquakes. What they would like to have are vocational skills, numeracy skills, basic language skills, so that they can go out and get a job and help, and in some cases, entirely support their family's financial needs. If we do not pay attention to this, we will never understand why our gripping videos of volcanic eruptions and earthquakes are not attracting them to the lesson.

Duration

Time management is one of the first things that a teacher learns. But often, the true meaning of duration is lost and it becomes a tool that merely helps us educators, pace our lessons so that we can complete the syllabus in time.

The true meaning of duration requires us to look at not just how long we have in the classroom, but what time the lesson is, which day of the week, perhaps even what came before and what will come after the lesson. Essentially, it means looking at time from the child's perspective, not ours.

Children have limited attention span, what that is, varies from child to child. Teachers are often taught that lessons should 'change frames' once every 10-20 minutes. But what is not made explicit is that each change of frame must still point the students back to the Key Learning that is to be acquired. Here is an example.

A teacher walks into class and spends 5 minutes introducing the suffix ~able. He takes 5 words and puts them in front of ~able and makes 5 new words. This takes another 10 minutes. He still has 20 minutes of the lesson to go. So he instructs the class to turn to page 25 of their workbooks and fill out the exercise by following the example given. The example reads thus;

> *Mary has bought a new dress that is **washable**.*
> *Washable: You can wash it.*

He now gives the class 10 minutes to complete this task and leaves the last 10 minutes for the checking of answers. The time passes, and during the checking of answers, he comes across this question.

> *We all agree that the play was **forgettable**.*
> *Forgettable:_____.*

He asks for a response from the students. A boy raises his hand,

"Sir, you can forget it."

What went wrong?

Before you put this down to inexperience, let me first caveat by saying that the teacher was a good teacher, a very experienced teacher. He genuinely cared for the students and took pains to ensure that the lesson was made up of different activities which would help the students change frames and sustain their interest. I know. I was that boy.

However, the error was this. The frames in the lesson were not teaching the use of the suffix ~able. In the first instance, it taught the students that if they put a word in front of the suffix, it creates the new word which the teacher wants. In the second instance, it taught the students that in order to complete the task given for the day, all they needed to do was to remove ~able from the highlighted word and insert the remaining word into a sentence which reads, 'You can *(insert root word here)* it.'

He also neglected the fact that the lesson was carried out in the middle of the afternoon, a time when students are bored and looking to get up to mischief. He also neglected to check the prior knowledge of the students, assuming that the topic was new to the class, not realising that he had a smart-alecky student with a rather good grasp of the language.

From here I hope you see how important understanding ***Subject, Level and Duration*** is to planning effective lessons. We need to understand the context in which we are trying to achieve the learning so that we can make the other aspects of the lesson more meaningful and therefore more effective.

Key Learning – Make learning a deliberate construct

I often cite the last example to illustrate what happens when learning is not made explicit. Learning will take place regardless of our efforts. What then becomes important is to ensure that the learning that takes place is in line with our desired goals.

Learning can also be a deliberate or an incidental construct. The same information, when delivered, can result in many different interpretations, and therefore different learning acquired. If we do not state point blank, in no uncertain terms, what the Key Learning is, what the truly important take away from the lesson is; our children will never know what to look out for. And this deliberate effort must start with the crafting of the Key Learning.

To this end, the structure that Wiggins and McTighe provide within the Understanding by Design framework affords us a comprehensive approach to the construction of relevant and meaningful learning experiences aimed at fostering long term retention of key knowledge.

Though there are 3 stages in the framework, in this chapter, we will focus on the 3 elements in Stage I to help us triangulate our goals and craft effective and meaningful Key Learning.

STAGE 1: IDENTIFY DESIRED RESULTS	
Enduring Understandings:	**Essential Questions:**
Students will be able to:	

Enduring Understandings – The Key Knowledge
Enduring Understandings can be interpreted as knowledge which is important for the children to acquire. Such knowledge should be meaningful to them long after they have stepped out of school. Be careful with what you select, for it can turn knowledge meant to be retained for 40 years to that which is retained for 40 minutes.

Let me illustrate using the previous example on plate tectonics.

Subject: Plate Tectonics (Volcanoes)

Here are 2 possible Key Learning that can be obtained from the subject description stated above;
'Volcanoes change the plankton population in the Atlantic.'
'Volcanoes change climates.'

Which Key Learning will you retain longer? Odds on, you'll remember that volcanoes change climates for much longer, because climate matters to more you than the Atlantic plankton population does, unless you are a blue whale, of course.

From this illustration, you will realise that that which is most meaningful to you, you will commit to the longest phase of your memory. The manner of knowledge is immaterial. The same piece of information, because it means different things to different people, will be retained in different phases of memory.

Take for example phone numbers. The same phone number, let's say Bob the grocer from 2 towns away, will hold different meaning for his wife, his children, his customers who rely on him for their supply of daily necessities and you, who haven't heard of him till now. No prizes for guessing who will be the first to forget.

In like manner, the same knowledge, when presented to children in different ways, will either encourage them to commit it to longer term memory, or not to pay any attention to it at all.

This means that when crafting learning experiences, we need to make sure that we present, not just the information, but the importance of the information to our children. And we can only do this effectively if we pay attention to *Subject, Level and Duration*.

Let us now see how being specific when defining the desired subject can us help craft even more meaningful Key Learning.

Subject: Plate Tectonics (Impact of Volcanoes on man)

By explicitly focusing on the impacts of volcanoes on man, the crafting of the Key Learning becomes even more direct. So for the child living far away from volcanoes, our Key Learning could be; *'Volcanic eruptions have regional and international implications.'*

With this, we could then look at the 2010 Icelandic eruption that brought travel in and around Europe to a standstill and have the children discover what happened, why it happened and how it happened. Better yet, if you have a friend who had his bicycle delivery date delayed by 4 weeks due to that volcanic eruption, using that personal anecdote may help to draw students into the intended learning even more.

By crafting Key Learning that is meaningful to the students, not only is knowledge about tectonic processes being acquired, when the students find interest in what they are learning, they are more likely to keep the knowledge in their long term memory.

Essential Questions – The Pathway to Knowledge

Once we have established the desired end-point for the learning experience, we then need to chart the course on which we are going to take the children. We can do this through the use of Essential Questions.

What are Essential Questions? Though Wiggins and McTighe define Essential Questions a little differently, for our purposes let us take Essential Questions to refer to any question, statement, or subsidiary knowledge that helps set mid-point markers to guide the acquisition of the intended Key Learning.

The function of Essential Questions is 2 fold. Firstly, it allows us to deliberately plan a sequence of experiences which allow the children to discover the knowledge for themselves. Secondly, it helps us build the bridge of meaning for the child from where they are, to where we want them to be. Let me give you an illustration.

I often see this poster on pub walls;
> *Those who drink get drunk.*
> *Those who get drunk go to sleep.*
> *Those who go to sleep do not sin.*
> *Those who do not sin go to heaven.*
> *So let's all drink and go to heaven.*

Putting aside the laughable message, the manner in which the argument is laid out is what I want to focus on.

From where we are, to where the author wants us to be, each statement progressively gives us a plausible reason for the subsequent stage of the argument, till at last the desired end point is reached. This is the essence of what we want to distil from concept of Essential Questions. Let me illustrate further.

Subject: Newton's First Law – Inertia
Level: 15 year olds of upper middle socio-economic standing
          Good family background
          Possibly having some background knowledge
Duration: 60 minute lesson at 9am in the morning, 1ˢᵗ period.

Let us assume that we are dealing with the dream class of students; bright, eager, able and fresh.

What might the Enduring Understandings be? How might we want to lead them to the intended Key Learnings?

In this example, there are several possible Key Learnings we could select. We could focus on the fact that forces are always trying to achieve equilibrium or we could focus on the fact that forces can be balanced or unbalanced.

Are the 2 concepts mutually exclusive or interrelated? If they ae interrelated, which is the greater of the 2? Will one lead to the other? If the understanding of forces being balanced, will lead to the understanding that all forces are trying to achieve equilibrium, then the former is the Essential Question, the pathway, whilst the latter is the Enduring Understanding, the end point.

Now we ask why they need to know this. Since they are able students, will we want to appeal to their desired career choices and make allusions to that? Will we want to appeal to their intellect and associate this key knowledge to deeper concepts more advanced than their syllabus in an effort to make them feel an even greater sense of achievement? Assuming we want to do the latter, we may set the Key Learning as;
'When forces try to achieve equilibrium, motion results.'

To lead them to that learning, we might use this series of questions;
'Why do things move?'
'How do objects start and stop moving?'
'How do forces start and stop objects moving?'

Once we have established this, we need to check if the pathway leads to the intended Key Learning. We do this by checking if answering the questions will lead the students to the intended Key Learning. If it will, then our job is done.

Essential Questions need not be presented as questions. It could be a series of problems to solve, or tasks to accomplish. Regardless of the form, they should be mid-point markers which help lead our children to the intended Key Learning.

'Students will be able to' – Evidence of Learning
Once we have established what we want them to learn and the path we want them to take, the next step will be to establish evidence of learning. What we would need to see in order for us to be convinced that the learning has successfully taken place.

To this end, it is important to be very deliberate about ensuring that what we want to see from our children matches the Key Learning that we want them to acquire.

If we go back to the story of my teacher and the suffix ~able, his desired student outcome was probably for his students to be able to complete the worksheet. However, he did not check to see if completing the worksheet actually helped his students acquire the intended Key Learning. So how do we do this?

We first determine if the Key Learning is **knowledge** or a **skill**. Then we craft an outcome that is **tangible** and **measurable**.

If the Key Learning is knowledge, we should find ways to showcase that knowledge, either by allowing for a presentation of the information acquired, or by allowing for the knowledge to be applied to different scenarios. The latter is preferred as it gives our children an additional avenue to see relevance of their learning in their lives and therefore increases the possibility that it will be committed to their long term memory.

But if the Key Learning is a skill, then we should find ways for the skill to be performed. Knowledge and skill are mutually exclusive entities and we should not mistake one for the other.

Here is an illustration.

Study Fig. 1 and answer the question that follows.

Food Consumption

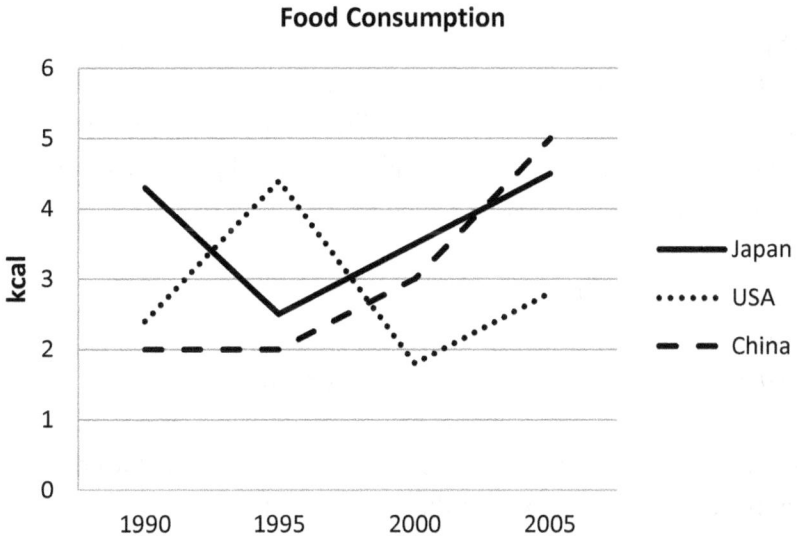

Fig. 1 Food Consumption in Japan, USA and China

Describe the changes in food consumption between 1990 & 2005.

This question checks for the child's ability to describe a graph, essentially the performance of a skill. So if used to compliment a lesson where the answering skills to Data Response questions was being taught, it would work perfectly.

However, if used in a lesson where the teacher wanted to check if students understood the reasons why food consumption varies from country to country, essentially knowledge, the command word will have to be changed from *'describe'* to *'explain'*. This would then require the students to produce reasons for the phenomena, which should reflect the extent to which the knowledge was acquired.

Once we have established the nature of the desired product, we can then craft the student outcome.

When phrasing the desired student outcome, we should take care to express it with tangible and measurable terms like *'complete the worksheet'*, *'give 3 examples of volcanoes'*, *'state the steps to bake a cake.'*. We should avoid intangible terms like *'understand'* and *'know'*. The more tangible and quantifiable the product is, the easier it will be to assess the success of learning.

Here is a simple illustration.
'Students will understand why volcanoes erupt.'
'Students will be able to describe the eruption process.'

Here are 2 statements pointing to the exact same knowledge, but it is much easier to determine the success of the latter.

One added advantage of making your student outcomes tangible and measurable is that your activities become much easier to plan.

When planning lessons, many of the teachers that I work with start by selecting the activity to be used in the lesson. Many neglect to establish the Key Learning nor do they chart out the course which they would like to take the children on, before deciding what tools they would like to use to help them on that journey. The end result is an activity, or a series of activities, that achieve little learning.

Through this discussion, I hope you see the importance of identifying the desired results we would like to see from our children BEFORE we look at activities. As long as you take deliberate action to understand your audience and then purposefully set out your desired goals, pathways and performance from the students, you will be able to construct effective and meaningful learning experiences for your children that will reside in their long term memory.

Exercise

For the subject, topic, area or skill of concern that you raised earlier, consider the following elements and fill out the table.

Subject:

Level:

Duration:

STAGE 1: IDENTIFY DESIRED RESULTS	
Enduring Understandings:	**Essential Questions:**
Students will be able to:	

Exercise - Analysis

Here are some things to consider about the various elements.

Subject:
- Were you specific when selecting the subject matter?

Level:
- What special circumstances do your students have?
- What steps are you taking to maximise the retention of Key Learning for your particular type of students?

Duration:
- How long is the lesson?
- Did your lesson change frames for the students?
- Did every frame point to the Key Learning for the lesson?
- Are there other extenuating time-related circumstances that will influence the lesson?

Enduring Understandings:
- Did you include knowledge that will stay relevant to the child long after the child leaves school?
- Is this knowledge complementary to the other pieces of information which the child is to acquire?

Essential Questions:
- Does the sequence of items bring the child to the desired Key Learning?
- Does the starting point require pre-requisite knowledge from the part of the child?
- Is it fair for us to expect that pre-requisite knowledge?

Student Outcome:
- Are we imparting knowledge or skill?
- Does the desired outcome require the performance of skill or the demonstration of knowledge acquired?
- How are we sure that if the child is able to demonstrate the knowledge or skill, they have acquired the Key Learning?

What would you have them do?

"Though the two sides of the same coin may look different, they both serve the same purpose and are worth just as much."

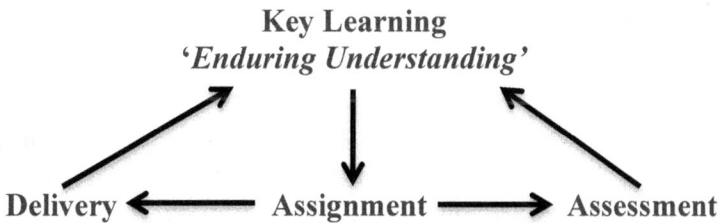

Key Learning
'Enduring Understanding'

Delivery ← **Assignment** → **Assessment**

In the previous chapters, we have been discussing the goals of learning. We looked at how we can establish Key Learning and Essential Questions for our children.

Setting the destination and charting the path on which we want to take our children in their journey of learning is the first step in ensuring that learning is meaningful, purposeful and will be retained in the long term memory.

In this chapter, we discuss the tools of learning, beginning with assignments and assessments. We will look at their importance and how they can be useful in measuring, guiding, and achieving long term retention of the intended Key Learning.

Purposeful assignments and assessments

Assignments, if constructed well, can reinforce, extend and allow for learning. They can be done under supervision, independently, collaboratively or individually. They can be conceptual in nature, or produce a tangible product.

Form notwithstanding, the non-negotiable is that they must forward the intended Key Learning and provide a platform on which to demonstrate the Desired Student Outcomes.

Assessments can also perform similar functions. Unfortunately, educators often use assessments only for gathering summative information. Sometimes, the information collected does not even inform on the success of the child's retention of the intended Key Learning. Instead, it merely measures how well the child can cope with exam-type conditions and questions.

In actual fact, assignments and assessments are like blanks in a metal press. They can be formed into any shape we wish, to serve any purpose we desire. They can even be used interchangeably. If we truly understand their versatility, we can harness their potential in crafting our learning experiences. Let me illustrate.

We start with a classic exam question as a root.
'Evaluate the success of measures to control deforestation.'

And assume the ideal classroom again.

Subject: Natural Vegetation – measures to control deforestation
Level: 15 year olds of upper middle socio-economic standing
Good family background
Possibly having some background knowledge
Duration: 60 minute lesson at 9am in the morning, 1ˢᵗ period.

Given the profile of our class, these could be the desired results;

STAGE 1: IDENTIFY DESIRED RESULTS	
Enduring Understandings: *The best efforts of any organisation are always limited by conflicts of interest between stakeholders.*	**Essential Questions:** *Why deforest? Why is it so difficult to curb deforestation?*
Students will be able to: *Identify the causes of deforestation. Identify the measures to curb deforestation. Identify the reasons that hinder their implementation. Explain why the implementation of the measures to curb deforestation is hindered.*	

Now let's think about the types of assignments that can be used.

A worksheet listing those exact student outcomes immediately comes to mind and would be the closest link between the learning experience and exam conditions. But what about others, such as a debate amongst stakeholders, a role play, writing a poem, a story?

The possibilities are endless, as long as they allow for a tangible and measurable performance. And because all of the possibilities can point the children to the Key Learning for this section, they can all promote long term retention of the key knowledge.

But not all possibilities will work for your class. Disadvantaged students would not be able to have as much access to out of textbook information and so may be more reliant on you to provide. Students less able in language may need more scaffolding to construct arguments. So from here, you see that there are many variables which influence the use of assignments

In our case, we may want to set for them a debate amongst stakeholders, grouping the class into expert groups and assigning each group a role. We then give them time in class to look up their relevant content area and prepare for the debate. Finally, we instruct them to centre their arguments on an agenda that looks at the effects of deforestation in a particular area.

We could even extend the activity by having them organize their verbal arguments into a written expose. In the end, they should end up with an argument that answers our root question.

Now, the root question no longer becomes an assessment in the way we expect assessments to be. And if we grade either the verbal argument, or the written expose, the assignment transforms into an assessment.

It is therefore important for us to realise that assignments and assessments are essentially two sides of the same coin. Though they may look different, they both serve the same purpose and are worth just as much.

Constructing and Measuring – Command Words and Rubric
In truth, our focus should not be on differentiating between assignments and assessments, but on how to use them as effective and accurate tools to measure our children's learning.

There must be a purpose to all assignments and assessments. The purpose, as mentioned, is always 2 fold;
- to bring our children back to the intended Key Learning; and
- to provide a platform on which to apply the Key Learning.

In order to accurately convey our purpose for the task, we employ the use of Command Words.

Command Words are essentially words and phrases we use to direct our audience to the intended task. Words like *'Describe'* and *'Explain'* tell our audience very explicitly what we want them to do in the exercise.

There are many types of Command Words and I deal with them at length in my book, *Understanding Questions*. But suffice to say in this discussion is that choosing the right Command Word for the task is like choosing the right tool for the job. An *'Explain'* when the intention was really to *'Evaluate'* will yield a very different product and hence an inaccurate reflection of the learning.

To measure the achievement of the child in meeting the demands of the Command Word, we need an accurate and appropriate rubric. The rubric must deliberately seek out and award positive performances of the Command Word so that the score is an accurate reflection of the degree to which the child has acquired the intended Key Learning. Let me illustrate.

Go back to the root question in our earlier example;
'Evaluate the success of measures to control deforestation.'

In this case, the rubric must allow for the performance of an appraisal and demand that the response examines the various perspectives of the issue, coming to a conclusion based on the arguments presented. Here is a good example;

Level 1
- Generalised answers with little support.
- Weak reasoning with many parts being unclear.

Level 2
- Only ONE SIDE of the opinion is given and supported with appropriate evidence, OR
- BOTH SIDES of the opinion are discussed, with weak support given for either or both.

Level 3
- Comprehensive answers supported by sound knowledge of theory and concepts.
- BOTH SIDES of the opinion are discussed and well supported with appropriate examples and evidence.

Conversely an answer scheme like the following will not measure the intended outcome stated in the question.
- Award 1 mark for each measure mentioned.
- Award 1 mark for each detail of the measure mentioned.
- Award 1 mark for each reason given to justify success.

When constructing the rubric, it is also important to pay attention to where we set the minimum acceptable level of achievement, put simply, the pass grade. The same task, when put to different groups of children, at different levels of learning, should not have the same minimum level of achievement.

For example, if we are introducing titration for the first time to a class of 7th Graders, it would not be fair for us to expect them to recount all the 7 steps to the experiment. We would give ourselves a pat on the back if they could remember the most important 3.

However, if the same task was now given to a class of 12th Graders, not only would we be expecting them to know the 7 steps, we would also expect them to include in their description, the possible errors that could result from each step.

This is what being accurate and appropriate means; able to measure the desired outcome; and able to offer a meaningful reflection of learning that is appropriate to level and circumstance.

Rubrics should also be tangible in their description. We should avoid unquantifiable descriptors like *'able to understand the audience'* or *'able to sustain the interest of the reader'*. If we can't put a finger on the demands of the rubric, it will lead to either our children seemingly never being able to attain that level of achievement, or result in large discrepancies between raters, all of which are not healthy to the education of our children.

In the end, assignments and assessments must be determined by the desired outcome. We need to be deliberate with the construction of the task so that not only can skills and knowledge be received and reinforced, the same skills and knowledge can be reviewed, revised and revisited during the post task analysis.

By leveraging on assignments and assessments, we will be able to quantifiably make learning more meaningful and hence improve long term retention for our children.

Exercise

For the desired outcomes that you identified in the earlier exercise, devise an assignment or assessment.

Subject:

Level:

Duration:

STAGE 1: IDENTIFY DESIRED RESULTS	
Enduring Understandings:	**Essential Questions:**
Students will be able to:	

Nature of task:

Collaborative or individual:

Desired Student Outcomes showcased:

Rubric for the task:

Desired Student Outcomes measured:

Interpretation of score:

Exercise - Analysis

Here are some things to consider.

Nature of task:
- Is this a timed test or homework?
- Why did you choose this task?
- How does this task complement your type of children?

Collaborative or individual:
- Is this group work or work done alone?
- Why did you select this mode?
- What future event or other purpose are you using this task to prepare your children for?

Desired Student Outcomes showcased:
- Which desired student outcome does this task showcase?
- Why only those or why all?
- How are they showcased?
- How do you know that you have been successful in providing the platform for those desired outcomes?

Rubric for the task:
- Does it measure the desired student outcome?
- How do you know?

Desired Student Outcomes measured:
- Which aspects of the outcomes did you measure?
- Why those?

Interpretation of score:
- What does your score mean?

How do we carry out the lesson?

"Don't do for the sake of doing."

When discussing learning and lessons, this is probably the part that is foremost on the minds of most educators, the activity. What we are going to do for the lesson; what activity we are going to run; what fieldtrip we are going to bring our children on; what experiment we are going to run in the lab today; are probably the first things that teachers think of when they plan for any lesson.

However, there is a reason why 'activity' only made it to the penultimate chapter of this book. It merely is a means to an end.

Activity-centric teaching - have we missed the point?
A conversation was overheard between two teachers.

"It's time to review the scheme of work again. I wonder what else we can do with it," said one.

"I hear the local repertory is staging Othello next year. I really want to go to that one. Can we please put that in?" said the other.

"Why not save the money and bring them when the international troupe comes to town?" replied the first.

Who can see what is wrong with that picture?

There is nothing wrong with bringing our children to the theatre to develop an appreciation for the arts or plays. It could even help them with their language.

However, the nature of the activity chosen must be grounded upon sound Key Learning that is matched with appropriate Desired Student Outcomes. How the lesson is carried out is really nothing more than a mere extension of what we want to achieve. Let me give you an illustration.

A math teacher wants to impart the concept of volume and wishes the Desired Student Outcome to be that his students are able to calculate the volume of various shapes. So he elects to bring into class a bar of Toblerone chocolate and a Ferro Roche.

The weather was hot that day, so by the time he got to class, the Toblerone bar and the Roche had both melted. He walks into class dismayed, saying,
"I had wanted to teach you the concept of volume today, but the chocolate I intended to use melted. So we shall instead carry on with practice sums."

Contrast this to his colleague who brought the same 2 items to class intending to run a role play in which the students would pretend they were bosses of chocolate factories trying to figure out which shape they should make their next big product into so that it would be the most economically viable to transport.

Which of the 2 do you think had a better idea of what purpose his chocolate bar was supposed to serve?

The activity must lend itself to the objectives of the lesson. The objectives must be constructed around the Desired Student Outcomes and intended Key Learning. We should never reverse engineer the process or it could lead to dire consequences.

That said, there are some things we must take note of when planning the learning activity.

The activity must take into consideration the audience
As discussed in earlier chapters, knowing the context in which our teaching is going to take place is extremely important. We need to consider aspects of our children that will affect their retention and attention, like what they would find important and meaningful.

If we are unaware of this, we will not be able to devise a suitable activity that would attract the children to the lesson; much like how using floral arrangement to teach vocabulary to the high school football team will be as fruitful as getting an elephant to break the quarter mile record.

The activity must give time for the desired outcomes
We must be deliberate in setting aside time for the demonstration of the desired outcomes. If we meant for the children to articulate arguments, then we should include time for a student-centred exposition, perhaps a viva. And we will know that we are on the wrong track if our lesson plan does not show time for it.

We also need to be realistic with what we want to achieve in our lessons. This is all the more crucial when we are faced with a short academic term and a long scheme of work and this where purposefully planning the Key Learning pays dividend.

Focusing on the larger Key Learning, can help us compress more learning into fewer learning activities. Let me illustrate.

Instead of setting aside one lesson each to cover land scarcity, water scarcity and fossil fuel scarcity, we adopt the larger Key Learning of *'resource scarcity is a real and present danger'*.

This will lead us to put in place one session where the class is broken up into expert groups, each looking at a particular aspect of resource scarcity. At the end of the lesson, the groups will share with the class, an information sheet which they put together on their particular area. This way, what took 3 sessions, now takes 1.

The activity must change frames
Children have limited attention spans. Even if the activity is something they enjoy, their attention will waiver if the time is not purposefully occupied. Therefore, every learning activity should have several frames. And we must ensure that each and every frame points the children back to the intended Key Learning.

The activity must be properly introduced
The introduction that needs to be done does not merely include the task to be completed, or the chapter to be covered, but the intended Key Learning and the Desired Student Outcomes.

Our children need to know, in no uncertain terms, what is expected of them and what they should be looking out for. Just like in the example of my teacher trying to teach suffixes mentioned in the earlier chapters, the class was not aware of what we were supposed to gain from the activity. Despite his best efforts, we, his students, still took to our own interpretation of the lesson and the Key Learning was never acquired.

Learning will take place regardless of what we do. We need to ensure that what is learnt is in line with what we want acquired.

The activity must be properly closed
Closure is a very important part of the learning activity. It not only sets the children up for the next thing to come, it more importantly it corrects any misconception the child might have developed in the lesson. By reiterating the Key Learning for the day, we will have the all-important opportunity to set right anything that might have been misinterpreted and such timely intervention will go very far in ensuring that knowledge is retained for the long term.

Regardless of the venue, the calendar or the circumstance, the intended Key Learning and Desired Student Outcomes should always guide the learning activity. Sometimes, the construction of the product could also become a learning activity.

That notwithstanding, the activity should never be allowed to dictate the learning. It is only a means to an end.

Exercise

For the Key Learning, Desired Outcomes and tasks that you have identified in the earlier exercises, construct a learning activity.

Subject:
Level:
Duration:
Key Learning:
Desired Student Outcomes:

Assignment/Assessment:

Time	Activity	Key Learning Covered	Desired Student Outcome
	Introduction		
	Main Activity		
	Closure		

Exercise - Analysis

Here are some things to consider.

How did the activity take into consideration the audience?

Did the activity give time to showcase the desired outcomes?

Did the activity change frames?

Were the Key Learning and Desired Outcomes introduced?

Was the activity properly closed?

How do we know if we succeed?

*"Mirror, mirror on the wall, have they failed,
or have I failed them all?"*

We have come to the end of this journey through education. The exercises in the book have also guided you through the process of constructing a meaningful learning experience that will encourage the long term retention of Key Learning.

So what have we learnt?

Learning occurs all the time
Our children are learning all the time. Everyone they come into contact with, either consciously or unconsciously, purposefully or inadvertently, teaches them something.

This also means that experiences are constantly being committed to their memories. Be it for the short or the long term, experiences are continually being etched into their lives.

Learning must be a deliberate construct
So if we want to leave our ideal experiences, our desired Key Learning and other such meaningful memories in their lives, we

need to be deliberate with the way we help them construct meaning from their learning.

We need to help our children distil, from their prescribed learning, the things that will be relevant and important to them long after they have left the learning experience, so that the right knowledge will be retained for the long run.

Everything must point to the Key Learning
To achieve this, every aspect of the learning process must point to the Key Learning to be acquired.

The Essential Questions, or mid-point markers that help us chart the course of their learning, should also purposefully bridge the gap from where they are to where we want them to be.

The Desired Outcomes should also give us some assurance that because they are able to apply the knowledge or perform the skills, they have indeed acquired the intended Key Learning.

The tasks given to reinforce and measure the acquisition should also be accurate and give meaningful feedback on their learning. They should assess based on rubric that is appropriate to the task, level and circumstance that our children are in.

The activity should also become the platform on which all the desired outcomes are realised. And we should always bear in mind that it should be the outcomes that drive the activity.

Understand the audience
Teaching cannot be done independent of the child. Therefore, understanding our children underpins our ability to achieve all that we have mentioned thus far. We need to be aware of what drives

them so that we can help them make the connection between their prescribed learning and their sources of motivation.

We also need to understand their circumstance and situation so that we can make meaningful and reasonable demands on them for their learning. By so doing, we hope that it will motivate them and increase the chances of long term retention.

Multi-disciplinary educators

Through this discussion, one thing that must have surfaced in your mind by now is that educators are increasingly called upon to become multi-disciplinary in ability and practice.

Our children are becoming increasingly varied in their interests and consequently in their drive. If we are to have any hope of giving them a meaningful education, not only must we help them make meaning of what we are teaching them, we sometimes have to help them draw the connections between our Key Learning and the learning they have received from other sources.

For example, in the chocolate factory owner role play mentioned earlier, the teacher had to be conversant with the importance of transportation costs in manufacturing. In the deforestation debate, the teacher would have to be familiar with the geopolitical situation of the country studied.

To compound the situation, not only must the teacher understand the concepts from areas not of his own, he must convey these concepts to the students in a manner that is accessible and yet not excessively time consuming since it is nonetheless still merely extra, out of syllabus knowledge that is being imparted.

We are therefore constantly walking the tight rope in the circus that is today's educational landscape, balancing the goal of education and the practical constraints of everyday life.

We succeed each and every time we decide to prioritise what is truly important, long term retention, over our own preferences and habits. By making the conscious effort to focus on helping our children retain Key Learning for the long term, we will be able to make learning more meaningful for our children.

www.ingramcontent.com/pod-product-compliance
Lightning Source LLC
Chambersburg PA
CBHW072036060426
42449CB00010BA/2294